West Chicago Public Library District
118 West Washington
West Chicago, IL 60185-2803
Phone # (630) 231-1552
Fax # (630) 231-1709

100-YEAR-OLD TUATARAS!

By Topper Evans

Gareth Stevens
PUBLISHING

Please visit our website, www.garethstevens.com. For a free color catalog of all our high-quality books, call toll free 1-800-542-2595 or fax 1-877-542-2596.

Cataloging-in-Publication Data

Names: Evans, Topper.
Title: 100-year-old tuataras! / Topper Evans.
Description: New York : Gareth Stevens Publishing, 2017. | Series: World's longest-living animals | Includes index.
Identifiers: ISBN 9781482456240 (pbk.) | ISBN 9781482456264 (library bound) | ISBN 9781482456257 (6 pack)
Subjects: LCSH: Tuatara–Juvenile literature.
Classification: QL666.R48 E93 2017 | DDC 597.9'45–dc23

Published in 2017 by
Gareth Stevens Publishing
111 East 14th Street, Suite 349
New York, NY 10003

Copyright © 2017 Gareth Stevens Publishing

Designer: Andrea Davison-Bartolotta and Bethany Perl
Editor: Ryan Nagelhout

Photo credits: Cover, p. 1 GordonImages/iStock/Thinkstock; pp. 2–24 (background) Dmitrieva Olga/Shutterstock.com; p. 5 Rudmer Zwerver/Shutterstock.com; p. 7 Mint Images - Frans Lanting/Mint Images/Getty Images; p. 9 Cameramannz/Shutterstock.com; p. 11 John Cancalosi/Photolibrary/Getty Images; p. 13 Honey Cloverz/Shutterstock.com; p. 15 Stuart Pearce/ Corbis Documentary /Getty Images; p. 17 KeresH/Wikipedia.org; p. 19 C. Allan Morgan/Photolibrary/Getty Images; p. 21 Oliver Strewe/Lonely Planet Images/Getty Images.

Printed in the United States of America

CPSIA compliance information: Batch #CW17GS: For further information contact Gareth Stevens, New York, New York at 1-800-542-2595.

CONTENTS

Boldface words appear in the glossary.

Living Fossils

Tuataras are one of the oldest species, or kinds, of animals in the world. Their **ancestors** lived with dinosaurs more than 200 million years ago! They're also some of the longest-living animals on Earth. Some people even call these amazing animals "living **fossils**."

Tuataras are spiny, greenish-gray **reptiles** that live on the islands of New Zealand. They look like lizards, but aren't. They're part of an animal group called Rhynchocephalia (rihng-koh-suh-FAYL-yuh). All other members of the group died out about 60 million years ago!

Sizing Them Up

Tuataras are pretty big reptiles. They're between 12 and 30 inches (30 and 76 cm) long. They weigh between 0.5 and 2.5 pounds (0.2 and 1.1 kg). Males are larger than females.

Three Eyes and Extra Tails

Tuataras have three eyes! Their third eye, called the parietal (puh-RY-uh-tuhl) eye, sits on top of the head. Scientists aren't sure what it does, and it gets covered in scales soon after tuataras are born. Like other reptiles, tuataras can also regrow their tail if it breaks off.

PARIETAL EYE

Growing Up

Tuataras grow until they're about 30 years old. They look for a **mate** when they're 10 to 20 years old. Males can mate every year, but female tuataras only mate every 2 to 5 years! It takes 12 to 15 months for tuatara eggs to **hatch**.

Night and Day

When tuataras are young, they're active during the day. As they get older, they start to go out at night. Scientists think this is to keep young tuataras away from older ones. Tuataras are cannibals, which means they'll eat other tuataras!

111-Year-Old Dad

In 2009, a 111-year-old male tuatara named Henry mated with Mildred, a female thought to be at least 70 years old. The two tuataras live in New Zealand at the Southland Museum and Art Gallery. Mildred then laid 11 eggs, and they all hatched!

HENRY

How Long Is Long?

Scientists say a tuatara may live up to 200 years. Some tuataras have even lived long enough to develop illnesses such as **cancer**. Henry, for example, had a cancerous lump removed from his body in 2002.

HENRY

19

Tuataras for the Future

Scientists think Henry may live up to 200 years! But not all tuataras are as lucky. The species is **endangered**, and many people are working to keep them safe. Tuataras need our help to last another 200 million years on Earth!

GLOSSARY

ancestor: an animal that lived before others in the family tree

cancer: a disease caused by the uncontrolled growth of cells in the body

endangered: in danger of dying out

fossil: the hardened remains of a plant or animal that lived thousands or millions of years ago

hatch: to break open or come out of

mate: one of two animals that come together to produce babies. Also, to come together to make babies.

reptile: an animal covered with scales or plates that breathes air, has a backbone, and lays eggs

FOR MORE INFORMATION

BOOKS

Greve, Tom. *Reptiles*. Vero Beach, FL: Rourke Publishing, 2012.

Hirsch, Rebecca E. *Tuataras: Dinosaur-Era Reptiles*. Minneapolis, MN: Lerner Publications, 2016.

WEBSITES

10 Fun Facts About the Tuatara
wired.com/2013/12/the-creature-feature-10-fun-facts-about-the-tuatara-or-just-the-tuatara-of-us/
Find out more about tuataras here.

Tuatara
animals.sandiegozoo.org/animals/tuatara
Learn more about tuataras at this San Diego Zoo site.

Tuatara: New Zealand's Living Dinosaur
media.newzealand.com/en/story-ideas/tuatara-new-zealands-living-dinosaur/
Find out about the tuatara's history in New Zealand here.

INDEX